I Can Count

Counting at Home

Rebecca Rissman

www.raintreepublishers.co.uk
Visit our website to find out more information about Raintree books.

To order:
☎ Phone 0845 6044371
▤ Fax +44 (0) 1865 312263
▧ Email myorders@raintreepublishers.co.uk

Customers from outside the UK please telephone +44 1865 312262

Raintree is an imprint of Capstone Global Library Limited, a company incorporated in England and Wales having its registered office at 7 Pilgrim Street, London, EC4V 6LB – Registered company number: 6695582

Text © Capstone Global Library Limited 2013
First published in hardback in 2013
Paperback edition first published in 2014
The moral rights of the proprietor have been asserted.

Edited by Rebecca Rissman, Dan Nunn, and Catherine Veitch
Designed by Steve Mead
Picture research by Mica Brancic
Originated by Capstone Global Library Ltd
Production by Alison Parsons
Printed in China

ISBN 978 1 406 24097 9 (hardback)
16 15 14 13 12
10 9 8 7 6 5 4 3 2 1

ISBN 978 1 406 24102 0 (paperback)
17 16 15 14 13
10 9 8 7 6 5 4 3 2 1

British Library Cataloguing in Publication Data
Rissman, Rebecca.
Counting at home. – (I can count!)
513.2′11-dc23
A full catalogue record for this book is available from the British Library.

Acknowledgements
We would like to thank the following for permission to reproduce photographs: © Capstone Global Library Ltd p. 23 (Lord and Leverett); Shutterstock pp. 5, 9 (© archidea), pp. 6-7 (© Dmitry Rukhlenko), p. 8 (© HelenaQueen, © Irina Rogova), p. 9 (© Nikolay Postnikov), pp. 10-11 (© jocic), pp. 12-13 (© 1000 Words Images), pp. 14-15 (© Africa Studio, © Eric Isselée), pp. 16-17 (© Artur Synenko), pp. 18-19 (© John Kasawa, © YaiSirichai), pp. 20-21 (© Alex Staroseltsev, © Obak), p. 22 (© Gelpi).

Front cover photograph of three stuffed animals in a bed reproduced with permission of Corbis (© Ocean).
Back cover photographs of a teddy reproduced with permission of Shutterstock (© Alex Staroseltsev), and a cake reproduced with permission of Shutterstock (© YaiSirichai).

Every effort has been made to contact copyright holders of any material reproduced in this book. Any omissions will be rectified in subsequent printings if notice is given to the publisher.

Contents

3

5

4

10

7

8

1

2

6

9

Can you count **one** front door?
It's painted red and blue.

5

Can you count **two** windows?
They're great for looking through!

7

Can you count **three** pairs of boots, lined up by the door?

Can you count **four** wet umbrellas, dripping on the floor?

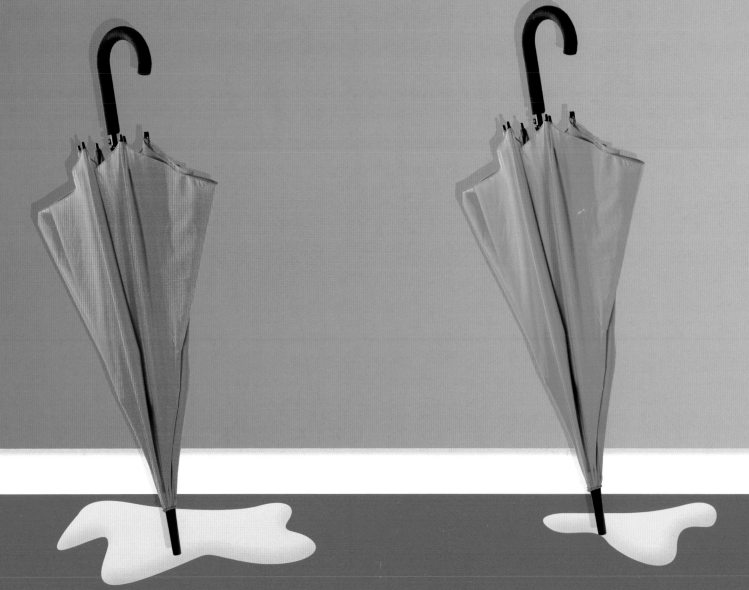

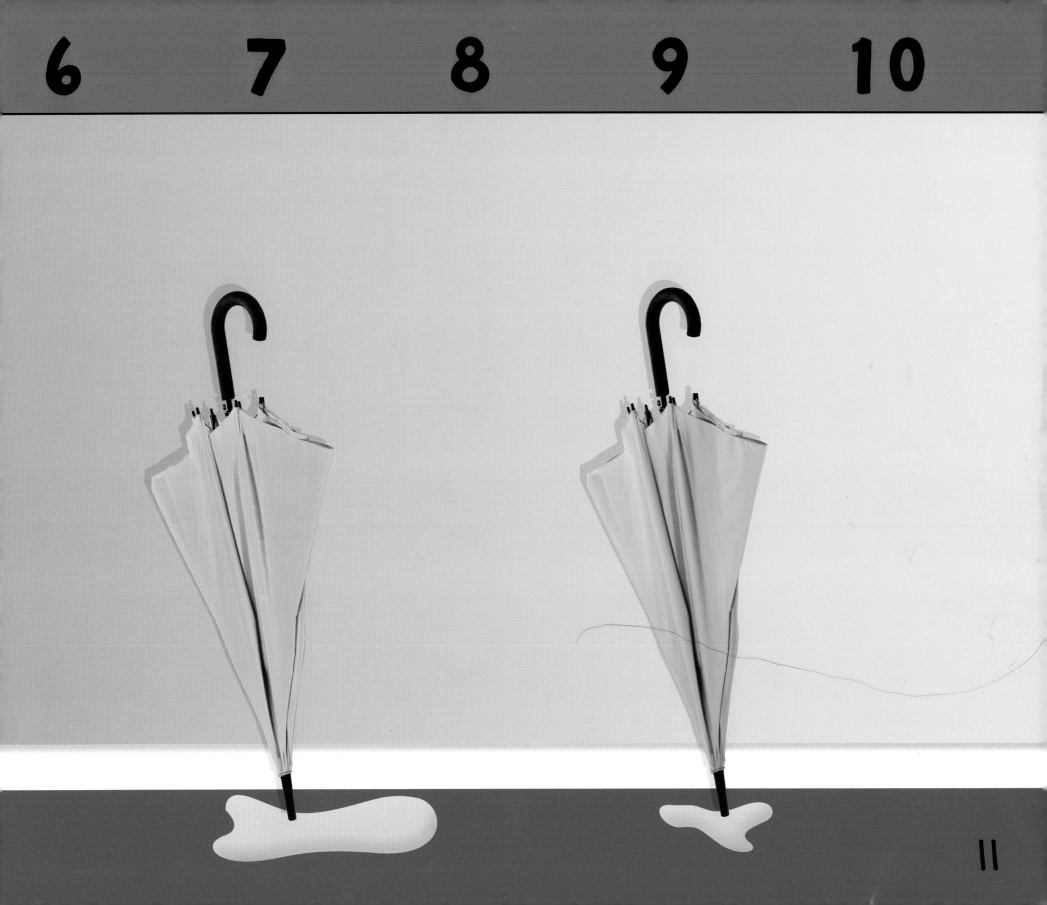

Can you count **five** wooden chairs, arranged around this room?

13

Can you count **Six** messy puppies? You'd better get the broom!

15

Can you count **seven** plates, set on this dinner table?

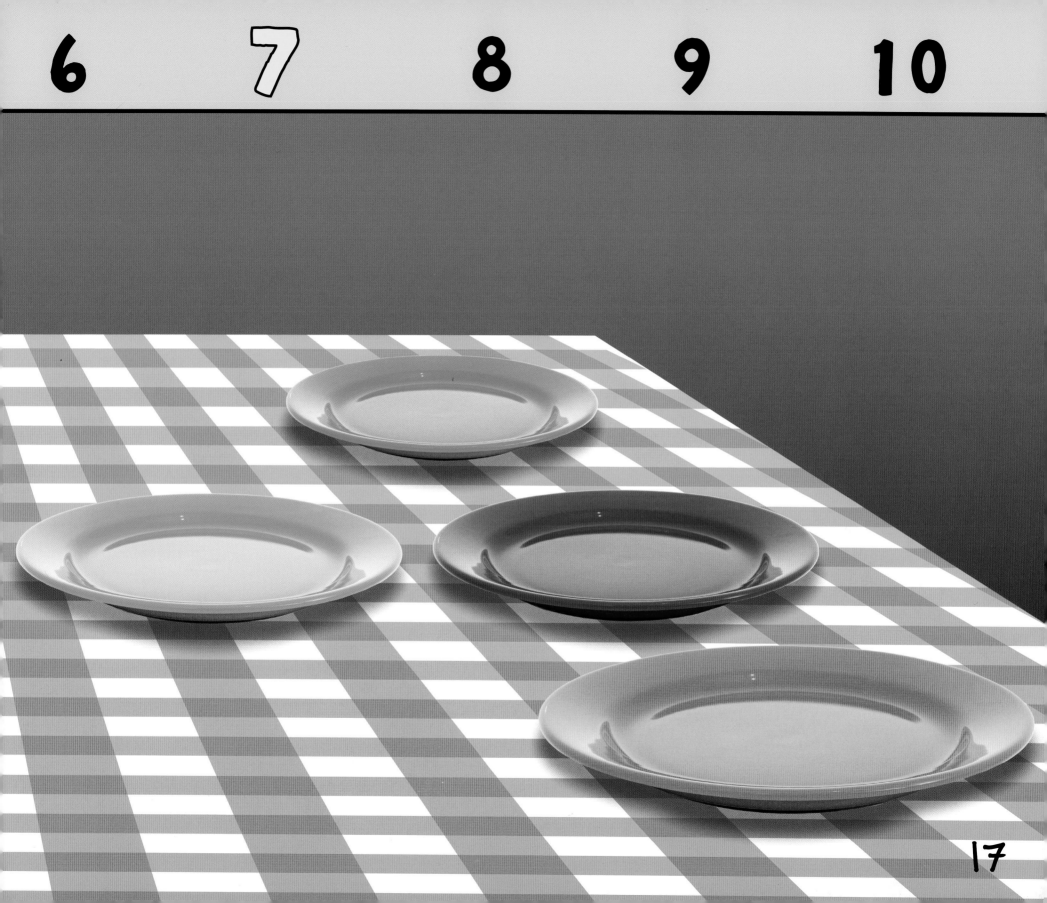

Can you count eight yummy cakes, to gobble if you're able?

Can you count **nine** teddy bears, resting on this bed?

Can you count **ten** different books,
with words to fill your head?

duck, egg,
ice ...

Guess the number
Which number comes next?

1, 2, 3, 4, ?   5, 6, 7, 8, ?

3, 4, 5, 6, ?   10, 9, 8, 7, ?

Index